The Freethinkers' Guide to the Educational Universe

A Selection of Quotations on Education

Educational Heretics Press exists to question the dogmas of education in general, and schooling in particular.

The Freethinkers' Guide to the Educational Universe

A Selection of Quotations on Education

Compiled by
Roland Meighan

Educational Heretics Press

Published 1994 by Educational Heretics Press
113 Arundel Drive, Bramcote Hills, Nottingham NG9 3FQ

Copyright © 1994 Educational Heretics Press

British Cataloguing in Publication Data

A catalogue record for this book is available from the British Library

Meighan, Roland

The Freethinkers' Guide to the Educational Universe

ISBN   0-9518022-4-0

Design and production: Educational Heretics Press

Printed by Mastaprint, Sandiacre, Nottinghamshire

Introduction

When I made the first selection of quotations on education in 1991 it was published under the title of *Unfashionably Unfascist?* Despite the long recession in the UK, now resulting in its twentieth or so recovery according to official sources, it sold out within months. It was enthusiastically received as a source book for discussions and also for illustrative material for lectures, lessons and seminars. Students also found the contents useful in the preparation of their essays on educational and related themes. Some resourceful people of a sharing disposition purchased multiple copies to give as presents to friends at Christmas.

In response to the comments and suggestions that were forthcoming from owners of the first compilation, which now appears to have the status of a collector's item, the new selection is produced in hardback for use as a library or classroom reference book, or as a coffee-table source book. Most of the quotations from the first book have been retained and augmented with additional ones so that the selection is twice the size of the original.

The quotations are again produced in large type to:

1. allow direct transfer to overhead projector transparencies,

2. to paste into lecture or seminar handouts,

3. to assist those of us with wearing eyesight to avoid searching for the magnifying glass.

I have immodestly yielded to suggestions to include a couple of quotations of my own, but I make no apology for increasing the number of gems from Bertrand Russell who, like Jeeves, in the admiring words of Bertie Wooster, "stands alone."

Roland Meighan

Shakespeare did not write with a view to boring school-children; he wrote to with a view to delighting his audiences. If he does not give you delight, you had better ignore him.

Bertrand Russell

* * * * *

The state which tries to use its power to exalt and promote the one kind of learning to the disadvantage of the other is an inhuman and barbarous state.

Enoch Powell

They work to pass, not to know: and outraged science takes her revenge. They do pass and they don't know.

Thomas Huxley

* * * * *

Education is not the filling of a pail, but the lighting of a fire.

W. B. Yeats

When you take the free will out of education, that turns it into schooling

John Taylor Gatto

* * * * *

What we want to see is the child in pursuit of knowledge, and not knowledge in pursuit of the child.

George Bernard Shaw

Education is a weapon, whose effects depend on who holds it in his hand and at whom it is aimed.

Joseph Stalin

* * * * *

... the boy must be transformed into the man; in this school he must not only learn to obey, but must thereby acquire a basis for commanding later. He must learn to be silent not only when he is *justly* blamed, but must also learn, when necessary, to bear injustice in silence.

Adolf Hitler

... the best learning happens in real life with real problems and real people and not in classrooms ...

Charles Handy

* * * * *

The most effective kind of education is that a child should play amongst lovely things.

Plato

Much of our expenditure on teachers and plant is wasted by attempting to teach people what they do not want to learn in a situation that they would rather not be involved in.

Colin Ward

* * * * *

It is the great triumph of compulsory government monopoly mass schooling that among even the best of my fellow teachers, and among even the best of my students' parents, only a small number can imagine a different way to do things.

John Taylor Gatto

**Nobody grew taller
by being measured.**

Philip Gammage

* * * * *

**When I was teaching in school, a man
came to a parents' meeting and
complained about the extraordinary
amount of testing we were doing. His
words went right to the heart of the
matter: "You're like a gardener who
constantly pulls his plants up by the
roots to see if they're growing."**

John Holt

No teacher ever said: 'Don't value uncertainty and tentativeness, don't question questions, above all don't think!' The message is communicated quietly, insidiously, relentlessly and efficiently through the structure of the classroom: through the role of the teacher, the role of the student, ... the 'doings' that are praised or censured.

Neil Postman and Charles Weingartner

* * * * *

We are faced with the paradoxical fact that education has become one of the chief obstacles to intelligence and freedom of thought.

Bertrand Russell

The schools ain't what they used to be and never was!

Will Rogers

* * * * *

Schools could become as obsolete as steam trains or paddle steamers.

C. Everett

School is the Army for kids. Adults make them go there, and when they get there, adults tell them what to do, bribe and threaten them into doing it, and punish them when they don't.

John Holt

* * * * *

... the army ... will be the last and highest school of patriotic education.

Adolf Hitler

My schooling not only failed to teach me what it professed to be teaching, but prevented me from being educated to an extent which infuriates me when I think of all I might have learned at home by myself.

George Bernard Shaw

* * * * *

Home-schoolers as a rule have no quarrel with teachers. My own parents are both teachers; I've seen a lot of work that teachers do, on their own time and out of their own pockets ... Our reservations are about the system of schooling, not the people who are doing their best within it.

British Columbia Home-schooler

Do not confine your children to your own learning for they were born in another time.

Old Hebrew Proverb

* * * * *

From my earliest memories of school (going back some 60 years) right up to the present, I am struck by how recurrent are the standard complaints and how little things change. Students are still locked into classrooms, still chained to desks, still herded through lessons that are far from reality and cruelly indifferent to individual differences in brains, background, talent and feelings.

Gene Lehman

Obedient children go willingly to the trenches.

Arthur Acton

* * * * *

Whatever their claims, schools are training most young people to be habitually subservient.

Chris Shute

Education is indoctrination, if you are white - subjugation if you are black.

James Baldwin

* * * * *

Of my two 'handicaps', being female put many more obstacles in my path than being black.

Shirley Chisholm

We can no more ordain learning by order, coercion and commandment than we can produce love by rape or threat.

Peter Jones

* * * * *

American kids like watching violence on TV and in the movies because violence is being done to them, both at school and at home. It builds up a tremendous amount of anger... The problem is not violence on TV. That's a symptom... The real problem is the violence of anti-life, unaffectionate, and punitive homes, and disempowering, deadening compulsory schooling, all presented with an uncomprehending smile.

Jerry Mintz

Every dogma must have its day.

Carolyn Wells

* * * * *

The prevention of free inquiry is unavoidable so long as the purpose of education is to produce belief rather than thought, to compel the young to hold positive opinions on doubtful matters rather than let them see the doubtfulness and be encouraged to independence of mind. Education ought to foster the wish for the truth, not the conviction that some particular creed is the truth.

Bertrand Russell

Thousands of caring, humane people work in schools, as teachers, and aides and administrators, but the abstract logic of the institution overwhelms their individual contributions. Although teachers do care and do work very, very hard, the institution is psychopathic; it has no conscience. It rings a bell and the young man in the middle of writing a poem must close his notebook and move to a different cell ...

John Taylor Gatto

* * * * *

Children are people; they grow into tomorrow only as they live today.

John Dewey

School is established, not in order that it should be convenient for the children to study, but that teachers should be able to teach in comfort. The children's conversations, motion, merriment ... are not convenient for the teacher, and so in the schools, which are built on the plan of prisons, ... are prohibited.

Tolstoy
* * * * *

There is nothing on earth intended for innocent people so horrible as a school. To begin with, it is a prison. But in some respects more cruel than a prison. In a prison, for instance, you are not forced to read books written by the prison warders and the governor.

George Bernard Shaw

We no longer have to force-feed education to children: they live in a world in which they are surrounded by educative resources. There are around 500 hours each of the schools' television and radio every year in this country. There are several million books in public libraries. There are museums in every town. There is a constant flow of cheap or free information from a dozen media. There are home computers which are easily connected to phones and thus other computers...There are thousands of work-places... There are... the old, the disabled, the very young all in need of children in their lives, all in need of the kind of help caring and careful youngsters can give, and all of them rich sources of information about the world, and freely available to any child who isn't locked away in school.

Richard North

The justification for school in its present form no longer exists.

Philip Toogood

* * * * *

Deep in my bones I remain convinced that ultimately it will be the deschoolers who are proved right, and that far in the future our descendants will view the whole concept of the school with mirth and disbelief.

Gerald Haigh

We may get our way but we don't get their learning. They may have to comply but they won't change. We have pushed out their goals with ours and stolen their purposes. It is a pernicious form of theft which kills off the will to learn.

Charles Handy

* * * * *

It used to worry me that, as a teacher, I was engaged in what was essentially microscopic fascism.

Chris Shute

Many parents I know put more hours into their golf games, or their wardrobes, or into accumulating enough capital for the purchase of unnecessary luxuries, than into their child's education. Because they are still children themselves, it simply does not occur to them to take an active role in their children's learning

David Guterson

* * * * *

There must be in the world many parents who, like the present author, have young children whom they are anxious to educate as well as possible, but reluctant to expose to the evils of existing educational institutions.

Bertrand Russell

Getting it wrong
is part of getting it right.

Charles Handy

* * * * *

Truth springs from argument
amongst friends.

David Hume

The current education system has been hijacked by reactionaries and the emphasis on academic subjects has produced education that is mediocre, generally exhausting and virtually worthless.

Mikell Billoki

* * * * *

... although home-schooling may work, it is by no means easy ... No-one should undertake to home-school without coming to terms with this fundamental truth: it is the fabric of your own life you are deciding about, not just your child's education.

David Guterson

The schools this country needs today must be institutions which abandon any and all attempts to limit the free pursuit of knowledge that every child, and every adult, engages in naturally, without any outside goading.

Daniel Greenberg

* * * * *

The spontaneous wish to learn, which every normal child possesses, as shown in its efforts to walk and talk, should be the driving force in education.

Bertrand Russell

Using school as a sorting mechanism, we appear to be on the way to creating a caste system, complete with untouchables who wander through subway trains begging and who sleep upon the streets.

John Taylor Gatto

* * * * *

To learn to know oneself, and to find a life worth living and work worth doing, is problem and challenge enough, without having to waste time on the fake and unworthy challenges of school - pleasing the teacher, staying out of trouble, fitting in with the gang, being popular, doing what everyone else does.

John Holt

Most criticism of the old education, and the old concepts it conserves and transmits, from Paul Goodman to John Gardner, makes the point that the students who endure it come out as passive, acquiescent, dogmatic, intolerant, authoritarian, inflexible, conservative personalities who desperately need to resist change in an effort to keep their illusion of certainty intact.

Neil Postman and Charles Weingartner

* * * * *

Our chief educational problem is deschooling schools, rather than deschooling society.

Roland Meighan

The skilled teacher, when a pupil is entrusted to his care, will first of all seek to discover his ability and natural disposition and will next observe how the mind of his pupil is to be handled ... for in this respect there is an unbelievable variety, and types of mind are no less numerous than types of body.

Quintillian on Roman Education

* * * * *

Whatever crushes individuality is despotism, by whatever name it be called.

John Stuart Mill

I believe that the computer presence will enable us to so modify the learning environment outside the classroom that much, if not all, the knowledge schools presently try to teach with such pain and expense and such limited success will be learned, as the child learns to walk, painlessly, successfully, and without organised instruction.

This obviously implies that schools, as we know them today, will have no place in the future. But it is an open question whether they will adapt by transforming themselves into something new or whither away and be replaced.

Seymour Papert

The new education has as its purpose the development of a new kind of person, one who - as a result of internalising a different set of concepts - is an active, inquiring, flexible, creative, innovative, tolerant, liberal personality, who can face uncertainty and ambiguity without disorientation, who can formulate viable new meanings to meet changes in the environment which threaten individual and mutual survival.

The new education, in sum, is new because it consists of having students use the concepts most appropriate to the world in which we all must live. All of these concepts constitute the dynamics of the question-questioning, meaning-making process that can be called 'learning how to learn'.

Neil Postman and Charles Weingartner

If personal quality is to be preserved, definite teaching must be reduced to a minimum, and criticism must never be carried to such lengths as to produce timidity in self-expression. But these maxims are not likely to lead to work that will be pleasing to an inspector.

Bertrand Russell

* * * * *

My grandmother wanted me to have an education so she kept me out of school.

Margaret Mead

The only real object of education is to leave a man in the condition of continually asking questions.

Tolstoy

* * * * *

Whatever an education is, it should make you a unique individual, not a conformist.

John Taylor Gatto

Education is a Good Thing because man has an insatiable appetite to learn and understand and because prominent amongst the joys that console him on his earthly journey is the joy of communicating to others, and especially to the young, what he has learnt and understood, and even more, how he managed to come by the learning and understanding.

Enoch Powell

* * * * *

The antithesis between a technical and a liberal education is fallacious. There can be no adequate technical education which is not liberal and no liberal education which is not technical.

Alfred North Whitehead

There is, I believe, actually nothing more powerful to say about education than this: that all people, however young or old, have an enormous drive and capacity to learn; that many aspects of typical schooling get in the way of this, partly by assuming that the reverse is true; that learners really start to explore and exercise their potential only as they take charge of their lives; that the most effective teachers trust learners, enhance their self-esteem, have no need to control them, provide an unconditional support which doesn't go too far, and value all types of intelligence in all areas of learning.

Paul Ginnis

**People must be educated once more
to know their place.**

UK Department of Education official
responsible for National Curriculum planning

* * * * *

**A school, like a fascist state, is about
the business of compelling people to
conform to a pattern of behaviour
and a way of thinking decided by the
few who hold power over them.**

Chris Shute

If you think education is expensive, try ignorance.

Derek Bok

* * * * *

Imagination is more important than knowledge.

Albert Einstein

Arithmetic ... is overvalued; in British elementary schools it takes up far more of the time than it should. The average man should be able to do accounts, but beyond that he will seldom have occasion for sums. What he may have learnt of complicated arithmetic will be of no more practical use to him in later life that would the amount of Latin he could have learnt in the same time ...

Bertrand Russell

* * * * *

The adults of today spent twenty-five hours of their young lives learning quadratic equations, with varying degrees of success. Was it time well spent?

Philip Gammage

Fundamentally, there is no right education except growing up into a worthwhile world. Indeed, our excessive concern with problems of education at present simply means that the grown-ups do not have such a world.

Paul Goodman

* * * * *

Either what is offered for learning must be experienced by the adolescents as illuminating, as informing their own life purposes, or it will be, at best, tolerated, and at worst, rejected.

James Hemming

A school should not be a preparation for life. A school should be life.

Elbert Hubbard

* * * * *

Minds are like parachutes: they only function when they are open.

Thomas Robert Dewar

School is a twelve-year jail sentence where bad habits are the only curriculum truly learned. I teach school and win awards doing it. I should know.

John Taylor Gatto

* * * * *

School is necessary to produce the habits and expectations of the managed consumer society.

Ivan Illich

Some true educational experiences are bound to occur in schools. They occur, however, despite and not because of school.

Everett Reimer

* * * * *

When we put together in one scheme such elements as a prescribed curriculum, similar assignments for all students, lecturing as almost the only mode of instruction, standard texts by which all students are externally evaluated, and instructor-chosen grades as the measure of learning, then we can almost guarantee that meaningful learning will be at an absolute minimum.

Carl Rogers

Assessment, more than religion, has become the opiate of the people.

Patricia Broadfoot

* * * * *

In examinations the foolish ask questions that the wise cannot answer.

Oscar Wilde

A child born in the U.K. stands a ten times greater chance of being admitted to a mental hospital than to a university ... we are driving our children mad more effectively than we are genuinely educating them.

R. D. Laing

* * * * *

The aim of education is to induce the largest amount of neurosis that an individual can bear without cracking up.

W. H. Auden

Do we create conflict by conditioning our children to pledge their allegiance, obey and defend their country without question? ... Or is he or she, by the very face of his or her commitment to and identification with the fragmented nationalistic view, paradoxically the enemy of peace?

Terrence Webster-Doyle

* * * * *

The disappearance of a sense of responsibility is the most far-reaching consequence of submission to authority.

Stanley Milgram

All sorts of intellectual systems - Christianity, Socialism, Patriotism etc., - are ready, like orphan asylums, to give safety in return for servitude. A free mental life cannot be as warm and comfortable and sociable as a life enveloped in a creed.

Bertrand Russell

* * * * *

School has become the replacement for church in our secular society, and like church it requires that its teachings must be taken on faith.

John Taylor Gatto

Show me a man who has enjoyed his schooldays and I'll show you a bully and a bore.

Robert Morley

* * * * *

Public schoolboys, whatever their particular school, ... had a language of their own ... ways and attitudes which they took for granted but which were foreign to me: for instance their acceptance of sodomy as more or less normal behaviour.

Malcolm Muggeridge

The starting point is wonder, curiosity and the joy of discovery, which external compulsion is more likely to extinguish than ignite.

Philip Coggin

* * * * *

The most beautiful thing in the world is, precisely, the conjunction of learning and inspiration. Oh, the passion for research and the joy of discovery!

Wanda Landowska

**I have never allowed schooling
to interfere with my education.**

Mark Twain

* * * * *

**Here is another curiosity to think
about. The home-schooling movement (USA) has quietly grown to a
size where one and a half million
young people are being educated
entirely by their own parents; ... the
education press reported the amazing
news that children schooled at home
seem to be five or even ten years
ahead of their formally trained peers
in their ability to think.**

John Taylor Gatto

It is heresy that education is useful, with the corollary that education produces economic well-being.

Enoch Powell

* * * * *

Civilisation is a race between education and catastrophe.

H. G. Wells

What the best and wisest parent wants for his own child, that must the community want for all of its children

John Dewey

* * * * *

... there can be no agreement between those who regard education as a means of instilling certain definite beliefs, and those who think that it should produce the power of independent judgement.

Bertrand Russell

The object of teaching a child is to enable him to get along without a teacher.

Elbert Hubbard

* * * * *

The things taught in school are not an education but the means of an education.

Ralph Waldo Emerson

A university is what a college becomes when the faculty loses interest in its students.

John Ciardi

* * * * *

Education with inert ideas is not only useless; it is above all things harmful.

Alfred North Whitehead

A child educated only at school is an uneducated child.

George Santayana

* * * * *

Two institutions at present control our children's lives: television and schooling, in that order.

John Taylor Gatto

Education is an admirable thing but it as well to remember from time to time that nothing that is worth knowing can be taught.

Oscar Wilde

* * * * *

The authority of those who teach is very often a hindrance to those who wish to learn.

Cicero

**Thank God I was never sent to school
To be flog'd into following the style of
a fool.**

William Blake

* * * * *

**No one who had any sense has ever
liked school.**

Lord Boothby

It follows logically from the banking notion of consciousness that the educator's role is to regulate the way the world 'enters into' the students. His task is to organise a process which already happens spontaneously, to 'fill' the students by making deposits of information which he considers constitute true knowledge. And since men 'receive' the world as passive entities, education should make them more passive still, and adapt them to the world. The educated man is the adapted man, because he is more 'fit' for the world. Translated into practice, this concept is well suited to the purpose of the oppressors, whose tranquillity rests on how well men fit the world the oppressors have created, and how little they question it.

Paulo Friere

The hard task of education is to liberate and strengthen a youth's initiative and at the same time to see to it that he knows what is necessary to cope with the ongoing activities and culture of society, so that his initiative can be relevant. It is absurd to think that this task can be accomplished by so much sitting in a box facing front, manipulating symbols at the direction of distant administrators. This is rather a way to regiment and brainwash.

Paul Goodman

* * * * *

Education is a state-controlled manufactory of echoes.

Norman Douglas

We must have some concept of the kind of person we wish to produce before we can have any definite opinion as to the education which we consider best.

Bertrand Russell

* * * * *

It is an iron law of education that rigid systems produce rigid people, and flexible systems produce flexible people.

Roland Meighan

It is absurd and anti-life to move from cell to cell at the sound of a gong for every day of your natural youth in an institution that allows you no privacy and even follows you into the sanctuary of your home demanding that you do its 'homework'.

John Taylor Gatto

* * * * *

... the 145 year-old system we are still trying to use after 145 years of failure must be scrapped and replaced. Small improvements, even if attainable, will not stave off collapse.

Leslie A. Hart

It is important that students bring a certain ragamuffin barefoot irreverence to their studies; they are not here to worship what is known, but to question it.

Jacob Brownowski

* * * * *

Education is a private matter between the person and the world of knowledge and experience, and has little to do with school or college.

Lilian Smith

Why should you mind being wrong if someone can show you that you are?

A. J. Ayer

* * * * *

Thought only starts with doubt.

Roger Martin Du Gard

This intelligence-testing business reminds me of the way they used to weigh hogs in Texas. They would get a long plank, put it over a crossbar, and somehow tie the hog on one end of the plank. They'd search all around till they found a stone that would balance the weight of the hog, and they'd put it on the other end of the plank. Then they'd guess the weight of the stone.

John Dewey

* * * * *

The lesson of report cards, grades and tests is that children should not trust themselves or their parents but should rely instead on the evaluation of certified officials.

John Taylor Gatto

People who can't think
are ripe for dictatorships.

Carl Rogers

$* * * * *$

What good fortune for those in power
that people do not think.

Adolf Hitler

If there is anything education does not lack today, it is critics.

Nathan Pusey

* * * * *

The trouble with the world is that the stupid are cocksure and the intelligent full of doubt.

Bertrand Russell

If a curriculum is to be effective ... it must contain different ways of activating children, different ways of presenting sequences, different opportunities ... A curriculum, in short, must contain many tracks leading to the same general goal.

Jerome Bruner

* * * * *

... good teaching is that which leads the student to want to learn something more.

Paul Goodman

In the long run of history, the censor and the inquisitor have always lost. The only sure weapon against bad ideas is better ideas. The source of better ideas is wisdom. The surest path to wisdom is a liberal education.

A Whitney Griswold

* * * * *

Education: that which discloses to the wise and disguises from the foolish their lack of understanding.

Ambrose Bierce

I deeply believe that traditional teaching is an almost completely futile, wasteful, overrated function in today's changing world. It is successful mostly in giving children who can't grasp the material, a sense of failure.

Carl Rogers

* * * * *

It's not that I feel that school is a good idea gone wrong, but a wrong idea from the word go. It's a nutty notion that we can have a place where nothing but learning happens, cut off from the rest of life.

John Holt

The wish to preserve the past rather than the hope of creating the future dominates the minds of those who control the teaching of the young.

Bertrand Russell

* * * * *

... our schools reflect our society closely, except that they emphasise many of its worst features.

Paul Goodman

But, good gracious you've got to educate him first. You can't expect a boy to be vicious till he's been to a good school.

'Saki' (Hector Hugh Munro)

* * * * *

The immediate case against compulsory school for adolescents is quite simply their barbarity: it is a triangle of hatred, humiliation and contempt.

Frank Musgrove

True education does not quiet things down, it stirs them up. It awakens consciousness. It destroys myth. It empowers people.

John Holt

* * * * *

The supreme end of education is expert discernment in all things - the power to tell the good from the bad, the genuine from the counterfeit, and to prefer the good and the genuine to the bad and counterfeit.

Samuel Johnson

Education ... has produced a vast population able to read but unable to distinguish what is worth reading.

George Macauley Trevelyan

* * * * *

My idea of education is to unsettle the minds of the young and inflame their intellects.

Robert Maynard Hutchins

Happiness in childhood is absolutely necessary to the production of the best type of human being.

Bertrand Russell

* * * * *

That children do not come to school by choice is another terrible indictment of our whole educational system.

John Kirkbride

There is no point ... in learning the 'answers' for very soon there will be different answers.

Paul Goodman

* * * * *

The chief object of education is not to learn things but to unlearn things.

G. K. Chesterton

The greatest challenges facing both the arts and education are how to navigate the perilous course between adventure and discipline; how to respond to tradition without either becoming its slave or rejecting it.

Robert Corrigan

* * * * *

Education is a method by which one acquires a higher grade of prejudices.

Laurence Peter

All my own work as a teacher and learner has led me to believe ... that teaching is a very strong medicine, which like all strong medicines can quickly and easily turn into a poison. At the right time (i.e. when the student has asked for it) and in very small doses, it can indeed help learning. But at the wrong times, or in too large doses, it will slow down learning or prevent it altogether.

John Holt

* * * * *

A boy will toil uphill with a toboggan for the sake of a few brief moments of bliss during the descent; no one has to urge him to be industrious, and however he may puff and pant he is still happy.

Bertrand Russell

I remember spending the greater part of my childhood wondering about adults. Were they ever children? From their behaviour toward children it seemed to me quite clearly that they could never have possibly been children.

Ashley Montague

* * * * *

... much of so-called 'discipline' is founded on unusual and extra-ordinary behaviour patterns which prepare children for nothing much. The result is either a rejection of all adult authority as meaningless, or a blind acceptance that it is adults or others who tell you what to do, and you need not work it out for yourself.

Lynn Davies

Schools have not necessarily much to do with education ... they are mainly institutions of control where certain basic habits must be instilled in the young. Education is quite different and has little place in school.

Winston Churchill

* * * * *

The education of today is nothing more than drill ... children must become accustomed to obey, to believe, to think according to the social dogmas which govern us.

Francisco Ferrer

I owe more to my ability to fantasise than to any knowledge I've ever acquired.

Albert Einstein

* * * * *

My optimism is based on the hope that public opinion will no longer tolerate the cover-up of child abuse in the name of child-rearing, once it has been recognised that ... child-rearing is basically directed not toward the *child's* welfare but towards satisfying the parents' needs for power and revenge.

Alice Miller

Education, the great mumbo jumbo and fraud of the age, purports to equip us to live and is prescribed as a universal remedy for everything from juvenile delinquency to premature senility. For the most part it only serves to enlarge stupidity, inflate conceit, enhance credulity and put those subjected to it at the mercy of brainwashers with printing presses, radio and television at their disposal.

Malcolm Muggeridge

* * * * *

To be caught up into the world of thought - that is being educated.

Edith Hamilton

Nothing in education is so astonishing as the amount of ignorance it accumulates in the form of inert facts.

Henry Adams

$* * * * *$

To the small part of ignorance that we arrange and classify we give the name Knowledge.

Ambrose Bierce

Why should we subsidise intellectual curiosity?

Ronald Reagan

* * * * *

... with the death of curiosity we may reckon that active intelligence, also, has died.

Bertrand Russell

By education most have been misled;
So they believe, because they were so bred.
The priest continues what the nurse began,
And thus the child imposes on the man.

John Dryden

* * * * *

We don't need no thought control.

Pink Floyd

The first problem for all of us, men and women, is not to learn, but to unlearn.

Gloria Steinem

* * * * *

The ultimate victory of tomorrow is democracy, and through democracy with education, for no people in all the world can be kept eternally ignorant or eternally enslaved.

Franklin D. Roosevelt

All to often, in debates about education, the basic questions are ignored in favour of mere technical issues. We should always begin by asking, 'What are we educating for?' 'What sort of people are we expecting to produce?' 'What kind of society do we envisage?'

Clive Harber

* * * * *

Children who are lectured to, learn how to lecture; if they are admonished, they learn how to admonish; if scolded, they learn how to scold; if ridiculed, they learn how to ridicule; if humiliated, they learn how to humiliate; if their psyche is killed, they will learn how to kill - the only question is who will be killed: oneself, others or both.

Alice Miller

... we must approach educational democracy carefully, so as to destroy in the process as little as possible of the valuable products that happen to have been associated with social injustice.

Bertrand Russell

* * * * *

Education today, more than ever before, must see clearly the dual objectives: education for living and education for making a living.

James Mason Wood

The only form of society which facilitates the continued evolution of the human species is a democratic form of society, and furthermore, the development of such a democratic society is dependent to a large degree on the democratisation of schools and schooling.

John Dewey

* * * * *

Democracy is not genetic. It is learned behaviour and it can equally be unlearned if education does not operate with democratic values, principles and methods.

Clive Harber

A teacher is one who, in their youth, admired teachers.

Henry Menken

* * * * *

An education enables you to earn more than an educator.

Anonymous

Not only do students in school spend very little time working together, but in many cases they are actually working against each other in competition for grades.

Susannah Sheffer

* * * * *

What the world now needs is not competition but organisation and co-operation; all belief in the utility of competition has become an anachronism. ... the emotions connected with it are the emotions of hostility and ruthlessness. The conception of society as an organic whole is very difficult for those whose minds have been steeped in competitive ideas. Ethically, therefore, no less than economically, it is undesirable to teach the young to be competitive.

Bertrand Russell

They know enough who know how to learn.

Henry Adams

* * * * *

Education is what remains when we have forgotten all that we have been taught.

George Halifax

The fact is that children are not naturally either 'good' or 'bad'. They are born with only reflexes and a few instincts; out of these, by the action of the environment, habits are produced, which may be either healthy or morbid.

Bertrand Russell

* * * * *

Why not make schools into places in which children would be allowed, encouraged, and (if and when they asked) helped to explore and make sense of the world around them ... in ways that most interested them?

John Holt

Any examiners' meeting where anxieties are expressed if there are 'too many' first class degrees will demonstrate the shallowness of any expressed national concern to raise overall standards of performance.

Lynn Davies

* * * * *

It is very difficult for people to believe the simple fact that *every persecutor was once a victim.* Yet it should be very obvious that someone who was allowed to feel free and strong from childhood does not have the need to humiliate another person.

Alice Miller

Break their wills betimes; begin this great work before they can run alone, before they can speak plain, or perhaps speak at all. Let him have nothing he cries for, absolutely nothing, great or small. Make him do as he is bid, if you whip him ten times running to effect it. Break his will now and his soul will live, and he will bless you to all eternity.

John Wesley

* * * * *

It is true for both pupils and teachers that degradation and humiliation alternate with "having a laugh": this is the unending dialect of school life, the alternation between laughter and soulless despair.

Frank Musgrove

Education extracts the active ingredient of living a full, inquisitive life, calls it 'learning' and then attempts to improve this learning through bureaucratic administration of curriculum.

Ivan Illich

* * * * *

... the government is making schooling the latest nationalised industry ...

Ian Lister

It is a good thing for an uneducated man to read books of quotations.

Winston Churchill

* * * * *

Whatever women do they must do twice as well as men to be thought half as good.   Luckily, this is not difficult.

Charlotte Whitton

The sum of human knowledge and the complexity of human problems are perpetually increasing; therefore every generation must overhaul its educational methods if time is to be found for what is new.

Bertrand Russell

* * * * *

It is better to understand a little than to misunderstand a lot.

Anatole France

What we can learn best from good teachers is how to teach ourselves better.

John Holt

* * * * *

When I look back at all the crap I learned in high school, it's a wonder I can think at all.

Paul Simon

Among all the leading figures of the Third Reich, I have not been able to find a single one who did not have a strict and rigid upbringing. Shouldn't that give us a great deal of food for thought?

Alice Miller

* * * * *

It gives us a very special, secret pleasure to see how unaware the people around us are of what is really happening to them.

Adolf Hitler

Dear Teacher,
I am a survivor of a concentration camp.
My eyes saw what no man should witness:

Gas chambers built by learned engineers,
Children poisoned by educated physicians,
Infants killed by trained nurses,
Women and babies shot and burned by
high school and college graduates.

So I am suspicious of education.

My request is: Help your students become
human. Your efforts must never produce
learned monsters, skilled psychopaths,
educated Eichmans.

Reading, writing and arithmetic are
important only if they serve to make our
children more human.

People whose integrity has not been damaged in childhood, who were protected, respected, and treated with honesty by their parents, will be - both in their youth and adulthood - intelligent, responsive, empathetic, and highly sensitive. They will take pleasure in life and will not feel any need to kill or even hurt others or themselves. They will use their power to defend themselves but not to attack others. They will not be able to do otherwise than to respect and protect those weaker than themselves, including their children, because they this is what they have learned from their own experience and because it is *this* knowledge (and not the experience of cruelty) that has been stored up inside them from the beginning. Such people will be incapable of understanding why earlier generations had to build up a gigantic war industry in order to feel at ease and safe in the world.

Alice Miller

Schools learned long ago that the way to keep children from thinking is to keep them busy.

Everett Reimer

* * * * *

It is in fact nothing short of a miracle that the modern methods of instruction have not entirely strangled the holy curiosity of inquiry; for this delicate little plant, aside from stimulation, stands mainly in need of freedom; without this it goes to wrack and ruin without fail.

Albert Einstein

... instead of a National Curriculum for education what is really needed is an individual curriculum for every child, within common guidelines maybe, but given expression in a formal contract between the home and the school.

Charles Handy

* * * * *

The only form of society which facilitates the continued evolution of the human species is a democratic form of society and furthermore that the development of such a society is dependent to a large degree on the democratisation of schools and schooling.

John Dewey

Sources

The quotations presented in this book have been collected over the years. The following books have been particularly fruitful in this task:

Charles Bufe *The Heretics Handbook of Quotations* See Sharp Press, San Francisco

Nicholas Bentley and Evan Esar *The Treasury of Humourous Quotations* J.M.Dent and Sons

J.B.Foreman *Collins Gem Dictionary of Quotations* Collins

John Taylor Gatto *Dumbing Us Down: The Hidden Curriculum of Compulsory Schooling* New Society Publishers

Jonathon Green *A Dictionary of Contemporary Quotations* Pan Books

Frank Muir *The Frank Muir Book* Corgi Books

Laurence Peter *Quotations for Our Time* Methuen

Bertrand Russell *On Education* and *Education and the Social Order* and *Sceptical Essays* and *Principles of Social Reconstruction* all published by Unwin

Chris Shute *Compulsory Schooling Disease* Educational Heretics Press

Index of Names

THEORY AND PRACTICE OF REGRESSIVE EDUCATION

by Roland Meighan

In the UK and the USA, there has been a sustained attack, for about twenty years, on something labelled 'progressive education'. The attack was, at first, tentative, then more confident, and then strident. In the 1988 Education Act and the various subsequent revisions, the attackers claimed victory. Yet the obscurity of the target makes the claim difficult to evaluate. There are two immediate problems. The first is what is meant by progressive education, and the second, what is the nature of what is supposed to replace it that is so superior. The opposite of progressive is regressive. **So the mystery investigated in this book is what is the nature of regressive education.**

The books shows how regressive schooling favours:
- tightly controlled learning, rather than eclectic and spontaneous enquiry,
- a set curriculum imposed by adults is preferable to a self-directed curriculum,
- the view that 'Life is no picnic, so school should be no picnic' so be fatalistic and endure it by getting toughened up,
- teaching being defined as formal instruction and authoritarian control,
- the idea that learning to work without pleasure in school ... is necessary to prepare to cope with the pain, frustration and dullness of employment - that is if you get any.

One feature of the return of more regressive schooling has been the emphasis on subjects and the imposition of these on younger and younger children. Yet subjects have only a modest part to play in the scheme of things: they are only part, and a diminishing part at best, of the tool kit of knowledge.

The conclusion is that the switch to regressive ideas in any schooling system is no more than an attempt to refine ancient machinery to try to make it more efficient in the pursuit of obsolete goals.

Professor Roland Meighan ...."has been studying and writing about new developments at the sharp end of innovation for a long time." (Damian Randle) With contributions by: **Professor Sir Hermann Bondi, Martin Coles, Professor Philip Gammage and Janet Meighan**
ISBN 0 9518022 3 2   Price £6.00

From: **Educational Heretics Press, 113 Arundel Drive, Bramcote Hills, Nottingham NG9 3FQ**

LIFELINES

by Ron Biggs

Six and a half years ago, I began to write down, in a notebook bought for the purpose, certain lines from the books I was reading. These lines presented me with valuable viewpoints on situations I was dealing with. From this six and a half year harvest, I have selected those which I would have most like to have known earlier in my life! They are also the ones I would most like to share with others seeking to make progress in their relationships with themselves and others. I have welcomed the insights of the many originators of the quotations I offer here and hope that the reader will find this varied selection to be truly food for thought and action. The collection includes such observations as:

If the teacher is indeed wise, he does not bid you enter his wisdom, but rather leads you to the threshold of your own mind.   Kahil Gibran

The wonderful thing about life is that there is no pass or fail situation. Life is just a learning experience.   Ramala

It's a common misconception that because we're alive we know how to live.
          Ayya Khema

Life is a flux. The intelligent person behaves according to the situation, the stupid according to ready made answers.   Bhagwan Shree Rajneesh

Are you really who you are, or are you what people have told you you are?
          Leo Buscaglia

If you can't be a sun, don't be a cloud.   Anon

Turn all your acquaintances into companions - if only briefly. Why not? They want companions too.   Ron Biggs

Price £5-00   ISBN 0-9518022-1-6

Educational Heretics Press,
113 Arundel Drive, Bramcote Hills, Nottingham NG9 3FQ

COMPULSORY SCHOOLING DISEASE

After twenty-five years as a modern languages teacher, Chris Shute, in his first book, presents his misgivings about schooling:
"I agreed to write this book because, after twenty-five years of school-teaching I became convinced that I was engaged in a form of microcosmic fascism."

"I intend to show in this book that schooling is, indeed, an activity which has aspects in common with fascism. That is not to say that teachers mean it to be so, or that they are conscious of the evil in which they are involved. Even fascism in its early phases attracted some reasonable, high-minded people who believed that the world could be changed for the better merely by the use of a little force and rigour in the right place."

"Perhaps their (my fellow teachers) true motivation was summed up for me by a lady colleague of mine some years ago. I had been talking to her about the grey, strained expressions I saw on the faces of my pupils as they went about the school. I suggested that it might be something to do with their feeling that they were not being educated so much as sentenced to hard labour for the crime of being children. She thought for a moment, and said in a grim voice: "I went through it. I see no reason why my child should escape.""

"I cannot bring myself to see education as she (my colleague) saw it, a life-long campaign against spontaneity, liveliness, and the natural energy of youth. Neither can I accept that the anger and frustration I saw in those children, which I now recognise as the same anger that slaves and occupied people feel, serves any good purpose in education."

"Home-based education or home-schooling is not discussed. This is not because I do not take it seriously as a method of educating children. In fact, I believe it is currently the best way to educate most children. But I hope that one day soon it will be possible for children to use schools as they should be used, as places where any person who happens to need help with their studies can go and receive it. Until that time, I must confine myself to commenting on schools as they are now, and challenging us to consider whether their regime contributes to enslaving the minds of children rather than setting them free."

ISBN 0-9518022-1-6   Price £6-00 from: **Educational Heretics Press**
113 Arundel Drive, Bramcote Hills, Nottingham NG9 3FQ

Education Now

EDUCATION NOW thinks that the word *education* has come to be misunderstood. Many people assume that it means 'what teachers do with children in school' and nothing else. **EDUCATION NOW** challenges that view. Its understanding of education is much wider, encompassing the many beneficial experiences which take place outside schools and colleges and which lead to valuable learning. It opposes those elements in the present system which promote uniformity, dependency, and often, a lasting sense of failure.

The vision of **EDUCATION NOW** includes:
- a focus on the uniqueness of individuals, of their learning experiences and of their many and varied learning styles
- support of education in human scale settings including home-based education, small schools, mini-schools, and schools-within-schools, flexischooling and flexi-colleges
- recognition that learners themselves have the ability to make both rational and intuitive choices about their education
- advocacy of co-operative and democratic organisation of places of learning
- belief in the need to share national resources so that everyone has a real choice in education
- acceptance of Einstein's proposal that *imagination is more important than knowledge* in our modern and constantly changing world
- adoption of the Universal Declaration of Human Rights in general and the European Convention for the Protection of Human Rights and Fundamental Freedoms in particular.

EDUCATION NOW maintains that people learn best:
- when they are self-motivated
- when they take responsibility for their own lives and learning
- when they feel comfortable in their surroundings
- when teachers and learners value, trust, respect and listen to each other
- when education is seen as a life-long process

EDUCATION NOW is a forum in which people with differing, diverse and undogmatic views can develop dialogue about alternatives to existing dominant and compulsory forms of education.
    Office: 113 Arundel Drive, Bramcote Hills, Nottingham NG9 3FQ

BOOKS BY EDUCATION NOW

Flexischooling by Roland Meighan £6-00
... a great pearl in his writings ... Professor Aleksander Nalaskowski

Never Too Late by John Holt £10-00
I applaud this book heartily ... Sir Yehudi Menuhin

Anatomy of Choice in Education Roland Meighan & Philip Toogood £10-00
...precisely what is needed to clear up present confusion and set coherent, purposeful, productive patterns for the future... Dr. James Hemming

Democratic Learning and Learning Democracy by Clive Harber £5-00
Democracy is the worst system of organisation - except for all the others!
Winston Churchill

Learning From Home-based Education edited by Roland Meighan £5-00
...the rich diversity of the home-based phenomenon is demonstrated.

Issues in Green Education by Damian Randle £5-00
... it certainly succeeds in provoking thought ... Chris Hartnett

Sharing Power in Schools: Raising Standards by Bernard Trafford £5-00
... our students are becoming more effective, self-confident and imaginative learners and workers. Examination results are improving ...

Early Childhood Education: Taking Stock
edited by Philip Gammage and Janet Meighan £5-00
This is essential reading for all involved in the education of young children.

Community Need and Further Education edited by Frank Reeves £10-00
The application of the principles of community education in a college of F.E.

Skills for Self-managed learning by Mike Roberts £5-00
This book reports on a ten year research study into this topic

Education Now, 113 Arundel Drive, Bramcote Hills, Nottingham NG9 3FQ

Beyond Authoritarian School Management:
the challenge for transparency
by Lynn Davies

Significant new trends are emerging in educational management internationally which threaten a return to authoritarianism but simultaneously offer possibilities for more open and democratic governance of schools.

Beyond Authoritarian School Management looks critically at four recent developments in the field of management in schools and colleges: comparative research on the realities of organisational life; the school effectiveness movement; equity and democracy initiatives; and school self-appraisal. In examining the various contemporary languages of management - from markets to militarism - the book exposes the power of managers to influence outcomes.

Lynn Davies argues for an institutional structure geared to the maximisation of rewards for all participants, arrived at through open investigation and experimentation. She concludes that the common thread is that the good manager is also a good researcher. The proposed model for school organisation is, therefore, that of a 'research park'. The headteacher becomes a research co-ordinator. Accepting that management training is a growing international endeavour, the book develops alternative training implications based on establishing performance indicators for transparency and democratic practice. The quest is open recognition of educational management as an essentially political activity. This book is designed for current or potential managers in schools and colleges, and all those concerned about the good governance of education.

This book is vital reading for anyone keen to move beyond the limitations of authoritarian management theory and practice into contemporary and more effective frames of reference.

Dr. Lynn Davies is Director of the International Unit of the School of Education at the University of Birmingham, UK.

ISBN   1-871526-16-7   Price: £10

Education Now Books
113 Arundel Drive Bramcote Hills Nottingham, NG9 3FQ

ALICE MILLER; THE UNKIND SOCIETY, PARENTING, AND SCHOOLING

by Chris Shute

Alice Miller wrote several books in which she revealed how, after many years as a practitioner of traditional psychoanalysis, she came to believe that she had discovered the true origin of the vein of ferocity which runs through human relationships everywhere. Her training had led her to assume that people become neurotic because they had not succeeded in resolving the conflicts with their parents resulting from their innate drives. It was only when she was able to detach herself from the Freudian presuppositions on which psychoanalysis is based and establish communication with her own childhood feelings that she realised a simple but revolutionary truth: people are not emotionally distorted by their unresolved Oedipus Complex, or by some complex mismanagement of their imperious, inescapable drives. Instead, it is the unrecognised cruelty of their parents, masquerading as 'firm discipline' and 'responsible control', which injects slow-acting poison into their lives.

Young children are utterly helpless. If their parents respect and respond to their inarticulate attempts at communication with the outside world by all the means in their power, well and good. But if they have learned from their own background and culture to believe that children are wicked and in need of repression, they will crush, 'for their own good', all their innocent attempts to act independently , leaving them angry, frightened, and frustrated. They will have learned that it is dangerous to resist the god-like power of their parents, and in the end they will solve their problems by the only means available to them: **they will forget the tragedy of their early years and grow up into a faithful imitators of those who oppressed them.**

Alice Miller's books convinced me that bad education (most modern education is bad because it is cruel and insensitive), painful child-rearing and political tyranny all have the same source: the well-nigh universal delusion that children do not feel, and that it doesn't matter what adults do to them. I want to encourage as many people as possible to read what Dr. Miller has written and to apply it seriously to their own thinking.

Price: £6-00   ISBN   1-9518022-5-9

Educational Heretics Press

113 Arundel Drive, Bramcote Hills, Nottingham, NG9 3FQ